P9-CFF-231

Contents

The Playmakers 4

Chapter 1: Birth of the Receiver 6

Chapter 2: Legendary Receivers 10

Chapter 3: Receiver Skills 16

Chapter 4: Stars of Today 32

Chapter 5: Future Star: You! 40

Record Book 44

Glossary 46

Find Out More 47

Index 48

Words in the glossary appear in **bold** type the first time they are used in the text.

The Playmakers

The players who catch passes are the big-play stars on a football team. They are the wide receivers and tight ends. These players help a team make first downs and score touchdowns. Here's a story of a receiver who was at his best with the game on the line.

WHAT A CATCH!

It was the fourth quarter of the final game of the 2007 season. The New England Patriots were trying to become the first team in 35 years to end a season undefeated. They trailed the New York Giants 28–23. Quarterback Tom Brady dropped back to pass. He threw a long, high pass down the field. Wide receiver Randy Moss **juked** past the defender and caught the ball at the Giants 22-yard line. Moss didn't stop running until he reached the end zone. Touchdown!

► Randy Moss shows perfect form as he catches a touchdown pass against the Giants.

GAME DAY: FOOTBALL

RECEIVERS

By Jim Gigliotti

Reading consultant: Cecilia Minden-Cupp, Ph.D.,
Literacy Specialist

Gareth Stevens
Publishing
CHILDREN'S LIBRARY

Please visit our web site at www.garethstevens.com.
For a free catalog describing Gareth Stevens Publishing's list of high-quality books, call 1-800-542-2595 (USA) or 1-800-387-3178 (Canada). Gareth Stevens Publishing's fax: 1-877-542-2596

Library of Congress Cataloging-in-Publication Data
Gigliotti, Jim.
   Receivers / by Jim Gigliotti.
     p. cm. — (Game day. Football)
      Includes bibliographical references and index.
     ISBN-10: 1-4339-1962-1 — ISBN-13: 978-1-4339-1962-6 (lib. bdg.)
     1. Wide receivers (Football)—United States—Biography—Juvenile literature.
     2. Wide receivers (Football)—United States—Juvenile literature. I. Title.
   GV939.A1G537   2010
   796.3320922—dc22[B]   2008055595

This edition first published in 2010 by
Gareth Stevens Publishing
A Weekly Reader® Company
1 Reader's Digest Road
Pleasantville, NY 10570-7000 USA

Copyright © 2010 by Gareth Stevens, Inc.

Executive Managing Editor: Lisa M. Herrington
Senior Editor: Brian Fitzgerald
Senior Designer: Keith Plechaty

Produced by Q2AMedia
Art Direction: Rahul Dhiman
Senior Designer: Dibakar Acharjee
Image Researcher: Kamal Kumar

Photo credits
Key: t = top, b = bottom, c = center, l = left, r = right
Cover and title page: Kevin C. Cox/Getty Images
Drew Hallowell/Getty Images: 4; Evan Pinkus/Getty Images: 5; Pro Football Hall of Fame/NFL/Getty Images: 6; George Marks/Retrofile/Getty Images: 7; Al Messerschmidt/The Sports Gallery: 8, 9t, 9b; Pro Football Hall of Fame/Getty Images: 10; Focus on Sport/Getty Images: 11; Darryl Norenberg/NFL/Getty Images: 12; Al Messerschmidt/The Sports Gallery: 13; NFL/Getty Images: 14; Darryl Norenberg/NFL/Getty Images: 15; Rob Tringali/Sportschrome/Getty Images: 16; G. Newman Lowrance/Getty Images: 17tl; Greg Trott/Getty Images: 17br; Kevin Terrell/Getty Images: 18; Tom Hauck/Getty Images: 19; George Gojkovich/Getty Images: 20–21; Scott Boehm/Getty Images: 22; Paul Spinelli/Getty Images: 23; G. Newman Lowrance/Getty Images: 24; Tom Hauck/Getty Images: 25t; Rob Tringali/Sportschrome/Getty Images: 26; Tom Hauck/Getty Images: 27, 28; Thomas E. Witte/Getty Images: 29, 30; Tim Umphrey/Getty Images: 31; Kevin Terrell/Getty Images: 32; Al Messerschmidt/The Sports Gallery: 33; Scott Cunningham/Getty Images: 34; Al Messerschmidt/The Sports Gallery: 35; Paul Spinelli/Getty Images: 36; Scott Boehm/Getty Images: 37; Tom Hauck/Getty Images: 38; Jeff Gross/Getty Images: 39; Mike Eliason: 40, 41, 42, 43; Kevin Terrell/Getty Images: 44; Wesley Hitt/Getty Images: 45.
Q2AMedia Art Bank: 7b, 25bl

Printed in the United States of America

1 2 3 4 5 6 7 8 9 14 13 12 11 10 09

Cover: Larry Fitzgerald of the Arizona Cardinals is one of the top receivers in pro football.

RECORD BREAKER

Moss's big catch covered 65 yards. The touchdown put the Patriots ahead. They went on to win the game 38–35. They finished the regular season with 16 wins and no losses. The catch also gave Moss 23 touchdown receptions for the season. That set a new National Football League (NFL) record.

Not every pass catcher can be a record setter like Randy Moss. However, every receiver's team counts on him. He needs to make big plays when his team needs them most.

◀ Randy Moss celebrates after the Patriots win over the Giants.

GLOSSARY

juked: made a fake that fooled a defender

CHAPTER 1

Birth of the Receiver

In the late 1800s, football was a game of brute strength. Teams moved the ball a few yards at a time by running into the middle of the **line of scrimmage**. Throwing a forward pass wasn't even legal until 1906!

MOVING WIDE

The early receivers weren't "wide" receivers at all. They were called "ends" because of where they lined up on the field. Most teams rarely threw the ball, so ends didn't catch many passes. That changed in 1935 when Don Hutson joined the NFL's Green Bay Packers. Hutson was so fast that the Packers split him wide to get him into open space. Receivers are still sometimes called "split ends."

DON HUTSON

THE FIRST TIGHT ENDS

Teams still needed someone on the end of the line to help block. That player became known as the tight end. For a long time, a tight end was only an extra offensive lineman. Tight ends blocked for running backs and helped protect the quarterback. However, tight ends were allowed to catch passes. Coaches found that they could cause problems for opposing defenses by using the tight end as a receiver.

▲ In the 1950s, many teams still bunched all 11 offensive players close to the line. Ends were mainly blockers.

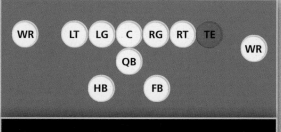

WR LT LG C RG RT TE   WR
QB
HB   FB

Key

WR: Wide Receiver
LT: Left Tackle
LG: Left Guard
C: Center
RG: Right Guard

RT: Right Tackle
TE: Tight End
QB: Quarterback
HB: Halfback
FB: Fullback

GLOSSARY

line of scrimmage: the imaginary line that divides the offense and the defense before each play

NEW RULES

In the late 1970s, the NFL wanted to make games more exciting. In 1978, the league put in new rules that made it easier to pass the ball. These rules included how linemen were allowed to block. They also included how **defensive backs** were allowed to guard receivers. The rules did what they were expected to do. Teams began passing the ball more than ever before. Receivers became a much bigger part of the offense.

Opening Up the Game

The numbers below are league-wide average yards per game per NFL team. See how the passing yards increased after the 1978 rules changes.

Year	Yards Passing	Yards Rushing
1977	141.9	143.9
1978	158.8	141.8
1979	180.4	135.6
1980	196.0	127.5
1990	194.8	113.9
2000	206.9	112.6
2008	211.3	116.0

▶ Dan Fouts of the San Diego Chargers was one quarterback who enjoyed the rule changes. He passed for more than 4,000 yards in three different seasons.

AIR CORYELL

Soon, wide receivers began posting amazing statistics. The San Diego Chargers offense was called "Air Coryell." It was named for Chargers coach Don Coryell. Wide receivers Charlie Joiner and Wes Chandler were stars of the offense. Tight end Kellen Winslow was also a favorite target of quarterback Dan Fouts. Winslow became one of the top pass-catching tight ends in the NFL.

WES CHANDLER

CHARLIE JOINER

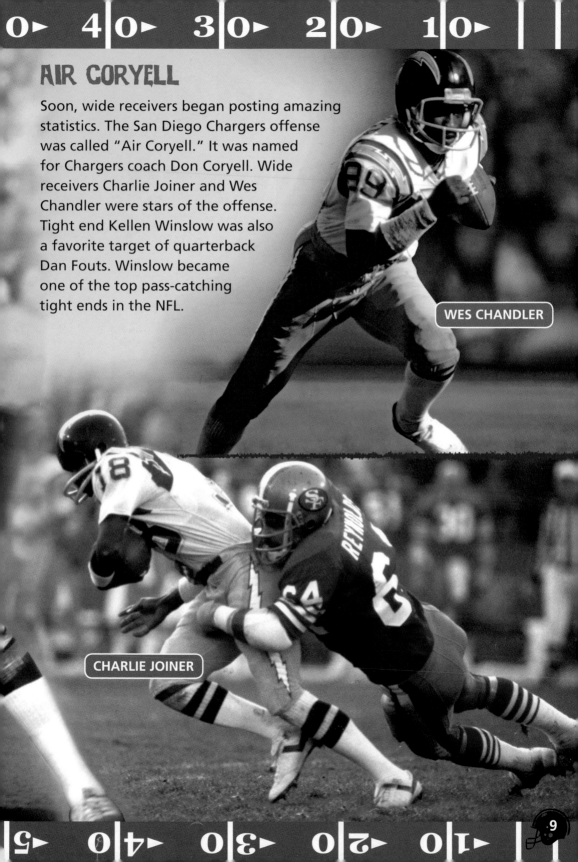

CHAPTER 2

Legendary Receivers

Meet some of football's greatest receivers— from the first superstar to the best of all time.

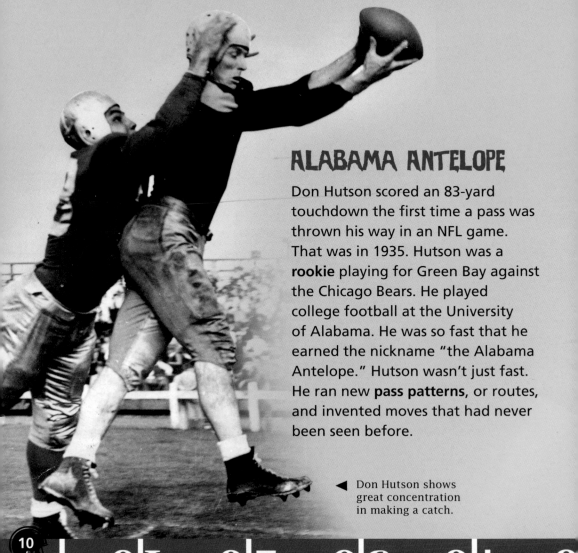

ALABAMA ANTELOPE

Don Hutson scored an 83-yard touchdown the first time a pass was thrown his way in an NFL game. That was in 1935. Hutson was a **rookie** playing for Green Bay against the Chicago Bears. He played college football at the University of Alabama. He was so fast that he earned the nickname "the Alabama Antelope." Hutson wasn't just fast. He ran new **pass patterns**, or routes, and invented moves that had never been seen before.

◄ Don Hutson shows great concentration in making a catch.

▲ Raymond Berry (82) makes a great one-handed catch. Few receivers had better hands than he did.

A Class by Himself

How much better was Don Hutson than everybody else during his career? In 1942, he led the league with 74 receptions. The next-best total was by Frank "Pop" Ivy of the Chicago Cardinals. He caught only 27 passes!

GLOSSARY

rookie: a player in his first season of pro football

pass patterns: the routes, or paths, that receivers run when going out to catch the ball

TWO OF THE BEST

Elroy Hirsch and Raymond Berry were different kinds of wide receivers. Yet they both became NFL legends. Hirsch played for the Los Angeles Rams from 1949 to 1957. He was flashy and exciting. His nickname was "Crazy Legs." Berry and quarterback Johnny Unitas were a great duo for the Baltimore Colts from 1955 to 1967. Berry wasn't flashy, but he was sure-handed. He practiced plays over and over until they were perfect.

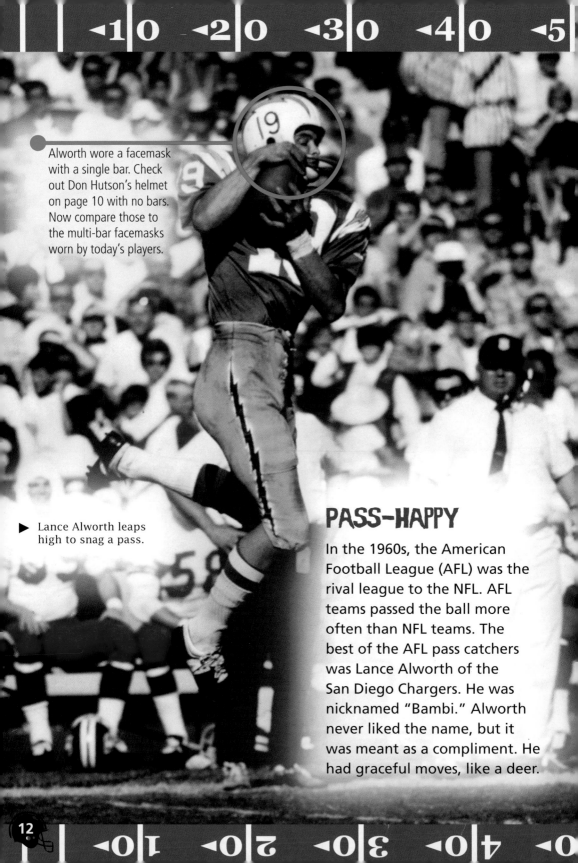

Alworth wore a facemask with a single bar. Check out Don Hutson's helmet on page 10 with no bars. Now compare those to the multi-bar facemasks worn by today's players.

► Lance Alworth leaps high to snag a pass.

PASS-HAPPY

In the 1960s, the American Football League (AFL) was the rival league to the NFL. AFL teams passed the ball more often than NFL teams. The best of the AFL pass catchers was Lance Alworth of the San Diego Chargers. He was nicknamed "Bambi." Alworth never liked the name, but it was meant as a compliment. He had graceful moves, like a deer.

THE ALL-TIME BEST

In 1984, San Francisco 49ers coach Bill Walsh was watching college football on television. He couldn't believe what he saw. A wide receiver from Mississippi Valley State was making catch after amazing catch. That wide receiver was Jerry Rice. The 49ers **drafted** Rice the next season. He went on to become the greatest wide receiver ever. Rice holds many major pass-catching records. They include most career receptions, yards, and touchdowns.

► Jerry Rice runs downfield after making a catch. His ability to make defenders miss tackles was one of his biggest strengths.

GLOSSARY

drafted: selected from the top college football players

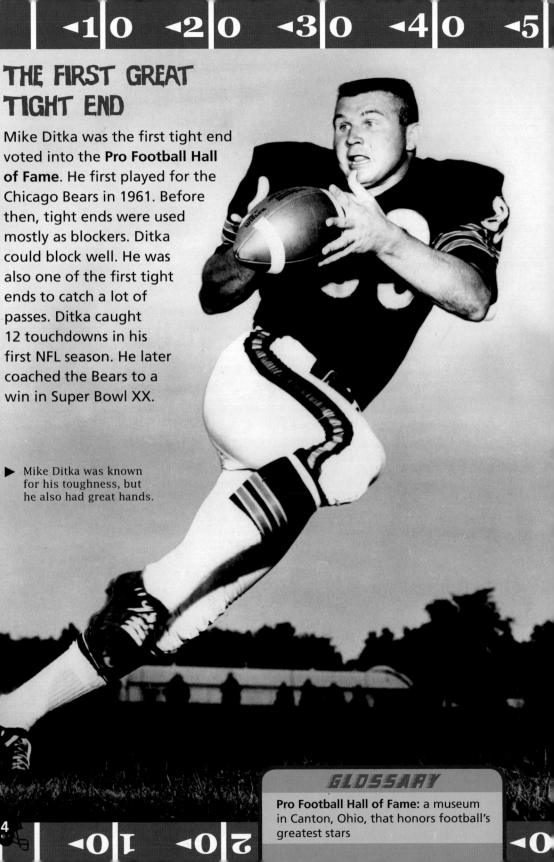

THE FIRST GREAT TIGHT END

Mike Ditka was the first tight end voted into the **Pro Football Hall of Fame**. He first played for the Chicago Bears in 1961. Before then, tight ends were used mostly as blockers. Ditka could block well. He was also one of the first tight ends to catch a lot of passes. Ditka caught 12 touchdowns in his first NFL season. He later coached the Bears to a win in Super Bowl XX.

► Mike Ditka was known for his toughness, but he also had great hands.

GLOSSARY

Pro Football Hall of Fame: a museum in Canton, Ohio, that honors football's greatest stars

MIGHTY MACK

The Baltimore Colts drafted John Mackey in 1963. Like Mike Ditka, he was a great receiver and a great blocker. However, Mackey brought another skill to the tight end position: speed. He scored long touchdowns because he could outrun defensive backs.

▼ John Mackey's size and speed made him very hard to tackle after he made a catch.

The Best of the 1980s

Mike Ditka and John Mackey helped pave the way for other top pass-catching tight ends. In 1979, the Chargers drafted Kellen Winslow. He went on to the Pro Football Hall of Fame. So did Ozzie Newsome of the Cleveland Browns. When he retired in 1990, only three NFL players—all wide receivers—had more catches than Newsome.

CHAPTER
3

Receiver Skills

What's the most basic skill needed to become a top receiver? Catching passes, of course! Here's how the pros do it.

THE LONG AND SHORT OF IT

Receivers catch passes all over the field. Some passes are short, near the line of scrimmage. Others are over the middle or near the sidelines on medium-length routes. Receivers are also part of the most exciting play in football: a **bomb** deep down the field. Each type of catch calls for different skills.

► Larry Fitzgerald of the Arizona Cardinals leaps to make a great grab.

GLOSSARY

bomb: a long, high pass that often leads to a touchdown

BASKET CATCH

A receiver tries to make a "basket" to catch the ball. The position of his hands depends on where the ball is thrown. If the ball is at or above the chest, the receiver's thumbs and index fingers should be touching. If the pass is below the chest area, the pinky fingers should be touching to create a different basket area.

◄ Calvin Johnson of the Detroit Lions shows good form while catching a low pass.

▲ Dwayne Bowe of the Kansas City Chiefs makes a basket with his hands for a high catch.

Catch in the Cradle

Receivers try to catch the ball by cradling it in the basket they create with their hands. They keep their hands away from their body. If a ball hits them in the chest first, it will likely bounce away.

Torry Holt keeps his eyes on the ball. The result? A touchdown!

ALWAYS READY

Good pass catchers don't just need proper technique. They also need focus. A receiver has to watch the ball all the way into his hands. That's not easy when he knows a defensive back is waiting to hit him! A receiver also has to focus on running his routes. That's true even when a play is not called for him. He needs to move the defense's attention away from his teammates. Also, he must be alert in case the quarterback decides to throw his way.

Speedy... or Quick?

The best receivers are speedy *and* quick. There's a difference between the two. Speed is how fast someone runs. Quickness means being able to promptly react and shift direction. Receivers need quickness to make sharp cuts to get open.

BIG AND SMALL

Wide receivers come in all sizes. Some coaches like pass catchers who are small and fast. Defenders have a hard time keeping up with smaller, speedy receivers. Other coaches like tall, strong wide receivers. Big receivers can outjump smaller defensive backs. They are also harder to tackle. Tight ends, though, have to be big. They are usually at least 6 feet 3 inches tall and 240 pounds. They have to be strong enough to block along the offensive line when needed.

▼ New England tight end Ben Watson (84) is six inches taller than his teammate, wide receiver Wes Welker (83).

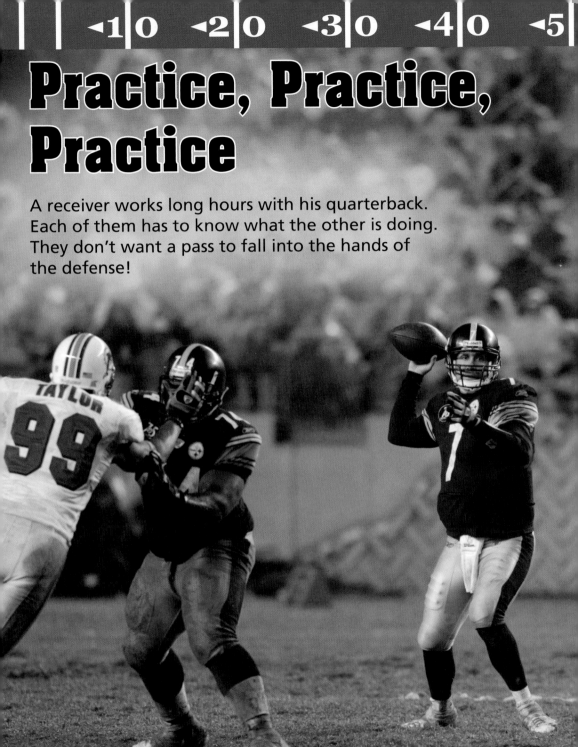

Practice, Practice, Practice

A receiver works long hours with his quarterback. Each of them has to know what the other is doing. They don't want a pass to fall into the hands of the defense!

TIMING IS EVERYTHING

A receiver can't just run to a spot and wait for the ball to come his way. A defender would be waiting there, too. He runs a route called by the quarterback in the **huddle**. The quarterback times his throw to arrive at the right spot at the same time that the receiver does. Sometimes, the ball is in the air before the receiver turns around to make the catch.

READING THE DEFENSE

Reading the defense means recognizing the type of coverage. Wide receivers and tight ends need to figure out where the defenders are going to be. They need to know if the defense is coming on a **blitz**. If it does, a receiver might have to block. On some blitzes, he might become the "hot" receiver. That is the player the quarterback has to throw to immediately.

◀ Receiver Hines Ward (86) of the Pittsburgh Steelers awaits a pass from quarterback Ben Roethlisberger (7).

GLOSSARY

huddle: the gathering of a team's players before each play

blitz: a rush of the quarterback by linebackers or defensive backs

◄ Bernard Berrian of the Minnesota Vikings takes a two-point stance. Putting one foot back helps him get a quick start.

Nearly all receivers wear gloves on both hands. The leather helps them grip the ball well in any weather.

A GOOD START

It's important for a receiver to burst off the line as soon as the ball is snapped. A wide receiver is usually in a two-point stance. He has two "points" on the ground—his feet! A tight end usually takes a three-point stance. The three points are his two feet and one hand.

BATTLE THE BUMP

A defensive player will try to "bump" a receiver as he comes off the line. Bumping is legal within five yards of the line of scrimmage if the ball has not been thrown yet. The receiver needs to be strong enough to fight his way past the defender. The receiver, of course, has a big advantage. He knows where he is going. The defensive player has to guess!

The Cutting Edge

When a receiver plants his foot firmly in the ground and changes direction, he is making a cut. Sometimes, he'll make two cuts on the same route. That's a "double move."

▲ Terrell Owens fights off an Arizona defender as he heads out on his pass route.

A LOT TO LEARN

In and outs. Posts and corners. Slants and drags. Curls and flies. A receiver can run many different pass routes. Each route is like a "branch" on a diagram called the **passing tree**. (See page 25.) The tree may look complicated, but the basic routes are easy to learn. Now, running those patterns with a defender in your face—that's hard!

▼ Dwayne Bowe (82) of the Kansas City Chiefs has an advantage over the defensive back. Bowe knows where he will run. The defender doesn't!

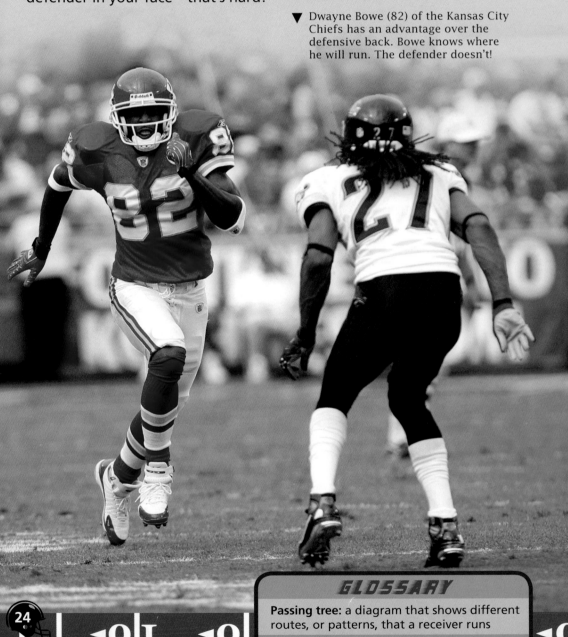

GLOSSARY

Passing tree: a diagram that shows different routes, or patterns, that a receiver runs

▼ DeSean Jackson of the Philadelphia Eagles catches a long pass on a fly pattern.

The Passing Tree

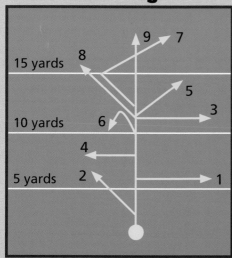

15 yards
10 yards
5 yards

9 7
8
5
3
6
4
2 1

THE NAME GAME

Some teams have different names for different routes. But all teams use the same basic passing tree. The goal is to let all players know where the receivers will be on each pass play.

Key

1: Quick Out   6: Curl
2: Slant   7: Post Corner
3: Deep Out   8: Post
4: Drag / In   9: Fly
5: Flag

On the Run

The best receivers don't just have great hands for catching. They also have great legs for running!

▲ Steve Smith of the Carolina Panthers turns on the jets to speed past a New Orleans Saints defender.

YAKKITY YAC

Sometimes, an announcer on television refers to a receiver's "YAC." That means "yards after the catch." The biggest playmakers usually have the highest YAC totals. Those receivers can catch the ball in the middle of many players and scoot around them. They can also catch the ball without breaking stride and keep on running.

HERE'S THE TRICK

Sometimes, a receiver gets the ball on a planned run. Usually, it's on a **reverse**. The receiver lines up as he normally would. At the snap, he loops behind the line of scrimmage. He takes a handoff from a teammate who is running toward him—and reverses the direction of the play. A receiver may also get the ball on an **end-around**. On that trick play, he takes a handoff directly from the quarterback. Both plays can really surprise the defense.

▶ Randy Moss (81) takes a handoff from the quarterback on an end-around.

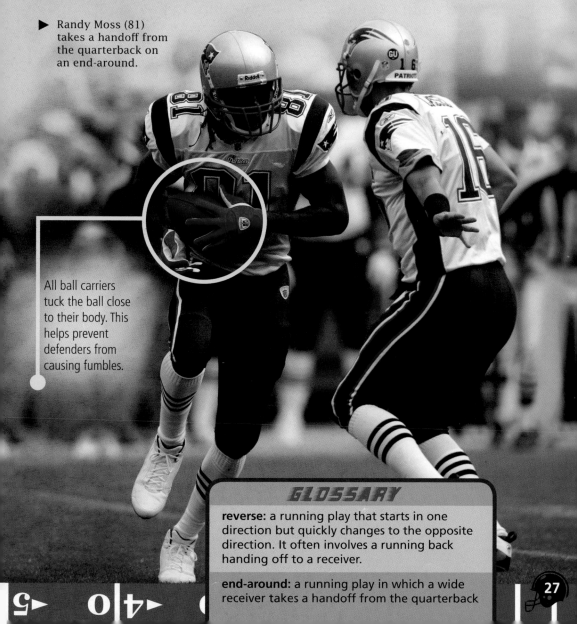

All ball carriers tuck the ball close to their body. This helps prevent defenders from causing fumbles.

GLOSSARY

reverse: a running play that starts in one direction but quickly changes to the opposite direction. It often involves a running back handing off to a receiver.

end-around: a running play in which a wide receiver takes a handoff from the quarterback

On the Block: Wide Receivers

Wide receivers don't just catch the ball or run with it. They have to block, too! The best blocking wide receivers are a big help to their team's running game.

HELPING HANDS

Sometimes, a running back breaks free for a big touchdown run. On those plays, some credit should usually go to a wide receiver. A key block from a wide receiver often helps spring a runner for a long gain.

▼ Donald Driver of the Green Bay Packers uses good form to block a defender.

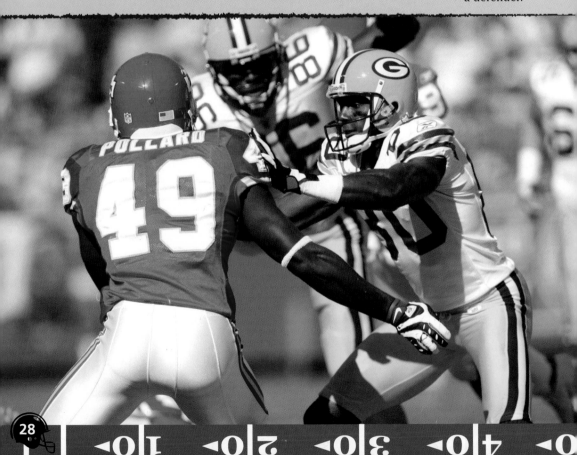

RUN SUPPORT

Receivers love to catch passes for touchdowns. But some also love to block. Receivers take great pride in making big hits on defensive players. A key block can charge up a team just as much as a big catch does!

▲ New York Jets receiver Jerricho Cotchery (89) makes a key block. Running back Leon Washington (29) is free to run for a big gain.

On the Block: Tight Ends

Today, tight ends are used in the passing game more than ever. However, they still have to know how to block.

IT TAKES TWO

Many teams have two players who share the job of tight end. One of them is usually used more often for pass plays. The other is used more often on rushing plays. Sometimes, teams have two tight ends in the game at the same time. A team usually does this when it is very close to the goal line or needs only a yard or two for a first down.

▶ The tight ends from the San Diego Chargers celebrate a touchdown. Brandon Manumaleuna (86) is a talented blocker. Antonio Gates (on his back) is a star pass catcher.

AN EXTRA OFFENSIVE LINEMAN

The five offensive linemen are the center, the two guards, and the two tackles. However, on many plays, the tight end is just like a sixth player on the line. On running plays, he uses the same blocking skills as an offensive lineman. On some passing plays, the tight end does not run a pattern. Instead, he protects the quarterback by blocking like the offensive linemen do.

▶ Tony Gonzalez (88) shows perfect blocking technique. A good blocker keeps his feet wide and his hands out in front of his body.

Best of Both Worlds

Most tight ends are either good blockers or good pass catchers. A tight end who is good at both is golden for an NFL team. Tony Gonzalez might be the best at doing both. He holds NFL records for most career catches, yards, and touchdowns by a tight end. After 12 seasons with the Kansas City Chiefs, Gonzalez joined the Atlanta Falcons in 2009.

CHAPTER 4

Stars of Today

We know what makes a good wide receiver or tight end. Now let's meet some of the best in today's NFL.

◄ Andre Johnson uses his strength to hold on to the ball against tough defenders.

TEXAS STAR

Andre Johnson of the Houston Texans is one of the NFL's best young receivers. In 2008, he led the league with 115 catches and 1,575 receiving yards. He also had eight touchdowns. Johnson's combination of speed, strength, and leaping ability make him very difficult to cover.

Three of a Kind

In 2008, the Arizona Cardinals boasted three outstanding receivers. Anquan Boldin, Larry Fitzgerald, and Steve Breaston each topped 1,000 receiving yards. The talented trio helped the Cardinals reach the Super Bowl for the first time ever.

ALL GROWN UP

When he was a youngster, Larry Fitzgerald was a ball boy at Minnesota Vikings games. Dennis Green was the team's head coach. In 2004, Green was the head coach of the Arizona Cardinals. He drafted the former ball boy that year. Fitzgerald has since become one of football's top wide receivers.

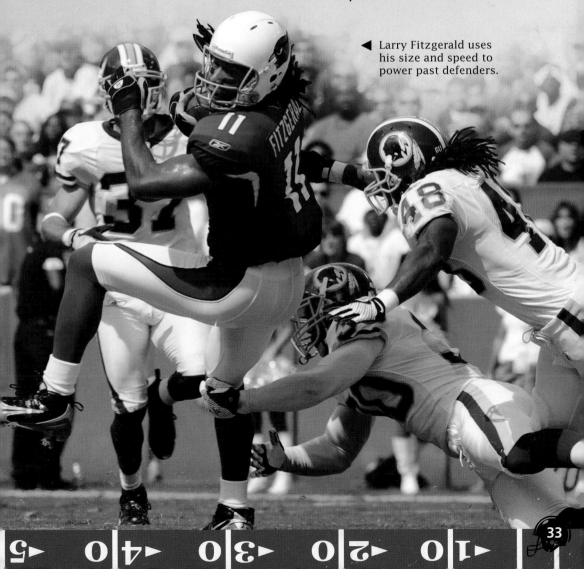

◀ Larry Fitzgerald uses his size and speed to power past defenders.

SMALL PACKAGES

They say that the best things come in small packages. That's true of Steve Smith of the Carolina Panthers. He is only 5 feet 9 inches tall. That makes him small for a football player. However, he is the best player in the NFL at gaining yards after the catch. His speed and great moves make him one of the toughest receivers to tackle. In 2008, he topped 1,000 yards for the fifth time in his career.

NO MORE SECOND FIDDLE

Reggie Wayne has been a solid wide receiver for the Indianapolis Colts for several years. However, he always played in the shadow of the great Marvin Harrison. In 2007, though, Harrison was injured. Wayne stepped up and has been quarterback Peyton Manning's main man ever since.

1,000 Club

Reggie Wayne's former teammate Marvin Harrison is one of the best wide receivers in NFL history. In 2006, Harrison became only the fourth player with 1,000 catches in his career.

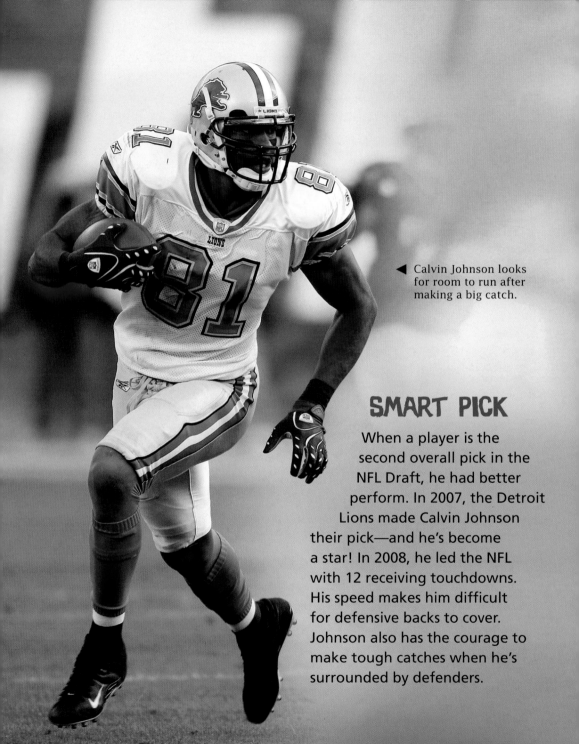

◀ Calvin Johnson looks for room to run after making a big catch.

SMART PICK

When a player is the second overall pick in the NFL Draft, he had better perform. In 2007, the Detroit Lions made Calvin Johnson their pick—and he's become a star! In 2008, he led the NFL with 12 receiving touchdowns. His speed makes him difficult for defensive backs to cover. Johnson also has the courage to make tough catches when he's surrounded by defenders.

DIFFERENCE-MAKER

Randy Moss has been an NFL star since 1998. But his career really took off after he was traded to New England in 2007. The Patriots offense improved from very good to all-time best. The 2007 Patriots scored more touchdowns (75) and more points (589) than any team ever. Moss scored 23 of those touchdowns and 138 of those points. In 2008, he topped 1,000 receiving yards for the ninth time in his career.

BIG MAN IN BIG D

Tight end Jason Witten is quarterback Tony Romo's favorite target for the Dallas Cowboys. Witten has a knack for getting open in the middle of the field. He also has great hands for making tough catches. Witten averaged more than 75 catches from 2004 to 2008. His career high came in 2007, when he had 96 receptions.

Like Father, Like Son

Kellen Winslow Jr. is the son of Hall of Fame tight end Kellen Winslow. Kellen Jr. was the top draft pick of the Cleveland Browns in 2004. In 2007, he made the **Pro Bowl** for the first time. He joined the Tampa Bay Buccaneers for the 2009 season. The younger Winslow is big, strong, and fast—just like his father!

GLOSSARY
Pro Bowl: the NFL's annual all-star game

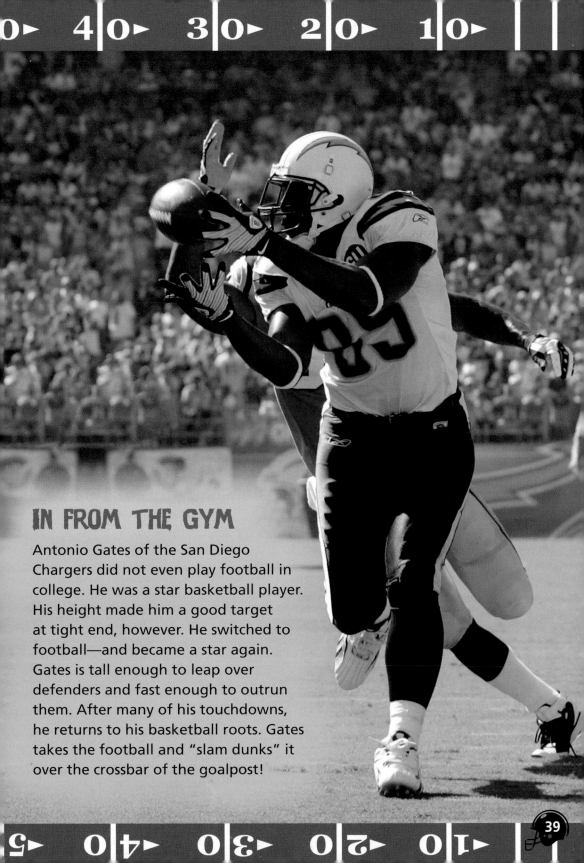

IN FROM THE GYM

Antonio Gates of the San Diego Chargers did not even play football in college. He was a star basketball player. His height made him a good target at tight end, however. He switched to football—and became a star again. Gates is tall enough to leap over defenders and fast enough to outrun them. After many of his touchdowns, he returns to his basketball roots. Gates takes the football and "slam dunks" it over the crossbar of the goalpost!

CHAPTER

5

Future Star: You!

Would you like to be a receiver? Here are some good ways to practice important skills.

LET'S PLAY CATCH

What's more fun than a game of catch with a friend? The best way to learn to catch is to practice over and over again. Soon, you won't even think about catching the ball. It will just come naturally. Remember to form a basket with your hands as you catch high or low throws.

▼ A young receiver makes a basket with his hands to grab a high throw.

TIMING PATTERNS

Pick a count. You can start with five. Run a route called by the quarterback. Count *one-two-three-four-five* while you are running. The quarterback counts at the same time you do. He throws the ball to the right spot. If your timing is right, the ball should arrive just as you do. This is great practice for the quarterback, too. A good quarterback and receiver spend hours working on their timing.

▶ Can you and the ball arrive at the same spot at the same time? Perfect timing takes a lot of practice.

Bad Is Good!

Don't worry if your quarterback doesn't throw a perfect pass all the time. Not every ball that comes your way in a game will be perfect. Hall of Fame wide receiver Raymond Berry used to have his wife throw him passes. Why? Because, he said, "No one threw bad balls better!"

GOOD POSITION

Good receivers use their bodies to help catch passes. You can practice this with some help. Have a friend throw short passes to you while another friend plays defense. Work on keeping your body between the defender and the ball. The timing you practiced on page 41 will help. Remember to practice good technique. Keep your eyes on the ball. Hold your hands away from your body. Catch the ball with both hands.

▼ Always keep your eyes on the ball and your hands away from your body.

Watch and See

The next-best thing to playing football is watching football. Go to a high school or college game near you. You can also check out games on TV. As you watch, pay special attention to the receivers. Watch how they run their routes. Watch how they block downfield. See what the tight end does on running plays and on passing plays. You can learn a lot just by watching!

ON YOUR TOES!

In the NFL, players must have both feet inbounds for a catch to count. In college, it's just one foot. A fun drill is to have your friend throw the ball above you as you are near a sideline. Try to catch the ball while keeping your toes on the field.

▶ Up on your toes! Stretch to catch the ball, but keep your toes on the ground.

Record Book

Who's the best of the best? Here are the top performers in some key receiving categories.

Wide Receiver Records

Receptions, Career
1. Jerry Rice: 1,549
2. Marvin Harrison: 1,102
3. Cris Carter: 1,101

Receiving Yards, Career
1. Jerry Rice: 22,895
2. Isaac Bruce: 14,944
3. Tim Brown: 14,934

Touchdown Catches, Career
1. Jerry Rice: 197
2. Terrell Owens: 139
3. Randy Moss: 135

Receptions, Season
Marvin Harrison, Colts: 143 (2002)

Receiving Yards, Season
Jerry Rice, 49ers: 1,848 (1995)

Receiving Touchdowns, Season
Randy Moss, Patriots: 23 (2007)

MARVIN HARRISON

* All records are through the 2008 season.

Tight End Records

Receptions, Career
1. Tony Gonzalez: 916
2. Shannon Sharpe: 815
3. Ozzie Newsome: 662

Receiving Yards, Career
1. Tony Gonzalez: 10,940
2. Shannon Sharpe: 10,060
3. Ozzie Newsome: 7,980

Touchdown Catches, Career
1. Tony Gonzalez: 76
2. Shannon Sharpe: 62
3. Dave Casper: 52

Receptions, Season
Tony Gonzalez, Chiefs: 102 (2004)

Receiving Yards, Season
Kellen Winslow, Chargers:
1,290 (1980)

Receiving Touchdowns, Season
Antonio Gates, Chargers: 13 (2004)

TONY GONZALEZ

Glossary

blitz: a rush of the quarterback by linebackers or defensive backs

bomb: a long, high pass that often leads to a touchdown

defensive backs: defensive players who are usually assigned to cover receivers

drafted: selected from the top college football players

end-around: a running play in which a wide receiver takes a handoff from the quarterback

huddle: the gathering of a team's players before each play

juked: made a fake that fooled a defender

line of scrimmage: the imaginary line that divides the offense and the defense before each play

passing tree: a diagram that shows different routes, or patterns, that a receiver runs

pass patterns: the routes, or paths, that receivers run when going out to catch the ball

Pro Bowl: the NFL's annual all-star game

Pro Football Hall of Fame: a museum in Canton, Ohio, that honors football's greatest stars

reverse: a running play that starts in one direction but quickly changes to the opposite direction. It often involves a running back handing off to a receiver.

rookie: a player in his first season of pro football

Find Out More

Books

Buckley, James Jr. *Eyewitness Football*. New York: DK Publishing, 1999.

Polzer, Tim. *Play Football!* New York: DK Publishing, 2003.

Stewart, Mark. *The Ultimate 10: Football*. Pleasantville, N.Y.: Gareth Stevens, 2009.

Web Sites

www.nfl.com
The official web site of the National Football League is packed with stats, video, news, and player biographies. Football fans will find all they need about their favorite players and teams here.

www.nflrush.com
It's the official kids' site of the NFL. Meet star players, see video of great plays, and get tips from the pros!

www.profootballhof.com
Find out more about the history of pro football and meet the legends of the game at the Pro Football Hall of Fame site.

Index

Alabama, University of 10
Alworth, Lance 12
Arizona Cardinals 16, 23, 33
Atlanta Falcons 31

Baltimore Colts 11, 15
Berrian, Bernard 22
Berry, Raymond 11
Boldin, Anquan 33
Bowe, Dwayne 17, 24
Brady, Tom 4
Breaston, Steve 33

Carolina Panthers 26, 34
Chandler, Wes 9
Chicago Bears 10, 14
Chicago Cardinals 11
Cleveland Browns 15, 38
Coryell, Don 9
Cotchery, Jerricho 29

Dallas Cowboys 38
Detroit Lions 17, 36
Ditka, Mike 14, 15
Driver, Donald 28

Fitzgerald, Larry 16, 33
Fouts, Dan 8, 9

Gates, Antonio 30, 39
Gonzalez, Tony 31
Green, Dennis 33
Green Bay Packers 6, 10, 28

Harrison, Marvin 35
Hirsch, Elroy "Crazy Legs" 11
Holt, Torry 18
Houston Texans 32
Hutson, Don 6, 10, 11, 12

Indianapolis Colts 35
Ivy, Frank "Pop" 11

Jackson, DeSean 25
Johnson, Andre 32
Johnson, Calvin 17, 36
Joiner, Charlie 9

Kansas City Chiefs 17, 24, 31

Los Angeles Rams 11

Mackey, John 15
Manning, Peyton 35
Manumaleuna, Brandon 30
Minnesota Vikings 22, 33
Mississippi Valley State 13
Moss, Randy 4, 5, 27, 37

New England Patriots 4, 5, 19, 37
Newsome, Ozzie 15
New York Giants 4
New York Jets 29

Owens, Terrell 23

Philadelphia Eagles 25
Pittsburgh Steelers 17, 21

Rice, Jerry 13
Roethlisberger, Ben 21
Romo, Tony 38

St. Louis Rams 18
San Diego Chargers 8, 9, 12, 15, 30, 39
San Francisco 49ers 13
Smith, Steve 26, 34

Unitas, Johnny 11

Walsh, Bill 13
Ward, Hines 21
Washington, Leon 29
Watson, Ben 19
Wayne, Reggie 35
Welker, Wes 19
Winslow, Kellen 9, 15, 38
Winslow, Kellen Jr. 38
Witten, Jason 38

About the Author

Jim Gigliotti is a freelance writer who lives in southern California with his wife and two children. A former editor at NFL Publishing, he has written more than two dozen books for youngsters and adults, including *Stadium Stories: USC Trojans* and kids' titles on football stars Tom Brady, Peyton Manning, and LaDainian Tomlinson.